WHISPERS OF THE CAULDRON

S MAYUR

Made with ♥ on the Notion Press Platform
www.notionpress.com

To those who find magic in the quietest places,
who hear the whispers in the shadows and transform them into dreams.
To the souls who embrace the unknown, who stir the cauldron of imagination,
and believe that every spark of wonder holds the power to light entire worlds.

This book is for the keepers of mystery, the seekers of truth,
and the dreamers who venture beyond the ordinary.
It is for those who find beauty in the dark,
hope in the silence, and endless possibilities in the stories yet to unfold.

May these words inspire you to see the world through enchanted eyes,
to weave your own tales of magic and meaning,

and may your heart forever burn with the fire of curiosity, courage, and creation.

Contents

Contents

Contents

Contents

Foreword

Whispers of the Cauldron is a poetic journey into the depths of the human experience, where the unknown stirs in the shadows, and the ethereal whispers call to those brave enough to listen. In these pages, the cauldron—both literal and metaphorical—becomes a vessel for transformation, a crucible where raw emotions, ancient mysteries, and personal revelations are forged into verse.

The poems within are not merely words on paper, but incantations that speak to the soul, inviting us to confront our innermost fears, desires, and dreams. Each piece is a reflection of the complex alchemy of life: the blend of joy and sorrow, love and loss, light and darkness. Through vivid imagery and haunting language, the poet creates a world where the mundane meets the mystical, and every thought seems to shimmer with a quiet power.

As you turn these pages, you may feel the warmth of the cauldron's fire or the chill of its smoke, but know that within these poems lies an invitation to explore the realms of imagination, emotion, and the subconscious. Whispers of the Cauldron is not just a collection of poems—it is an invitation to listen to the quiet calls that echo in the depths of our hearts and minds. May it lead you to places both familiar and foreign, where every whisper holds a world of meaning.

Preface

In the stillness of ancient woods, where the trees weave tales of forgotten magic, and beneath the silvered glow of a waxing moon, there exists a world where the ordinary transforms into the extraordinary. Whispers of the Cauldron invites you into this world, where every verse carries the weight of spells, secrets, and the timeless dance between light and shadow.

This collection is not merely a book of poems; it is a gateway, a cauldron brimming with the essence of emotions, dreams, and the unexplored realms of the human spirit. Each poem is a stirring incantation, carefully crafted to stir the depths of your imagination, and perhaps, awaken something long dormant within your soul. The cauldron itself is a symbol of transformation—a vessel where elements of sorrow, joy, fear, and love are mixed together, creating something new, something profoundly beautiful.

As you turn the pages, listen closely to the whispers within these words. They carry with them the voices of ancestors long passed, the echoes of forgotten times, and the promise of magic yet to unfold. Whether you seek solace or adventure, Whispers of the Cauldron is here to guide you through uncharted waters, to challenge your perceptions, and to remind you of the mysticism that lies in the quietest moments of life.

Welcome to a world where the cauldron bubbles, and the whispers never cease.

Acknowledgements

would like to express my heartfelt gratitude to everyone who has contributed to the creation of Whispers of the Cauldron.

To my family, for their unwavering support and encouragement, which has always fueled my passion and determination. Your belief in me has been a constant source of strength.

To my friends, who offered their valuable insights, feedback, and kindness, helping me shape this story into something truly special. Your words of wisdom have been a guiding light.

To all the readers who embark on this journey with me your enthusiasm and support mean the world. Without you, this story would not have found its place in the world.

Lastly, to the dreamers, the creators, and the wanderers who continue to inspire me daily. This book is for you.

Thank you all for your love, belief, and support.

{S Mayur}

Prologue

In the stillness of twilight, where the last light flickers and fades,
The cauldron stirs with a pulse, its voice a symphony of forgotten secrets,
Whispers rising like smoke from its ancient depths, curling into the ears of dreamers,
Carrying fragments of truths lost to time, of fears left unspoken, of desires unquenched.
Each whisper a murmur of the past, each note a song for the souls who listen.
This book is not mere ink upon paper,
But a vessel of alchemy, transmuting simple words into powerful spells,
Each line a ritual, each word a spark, each verse a potion brewed with longing,
Each stanza a charm cast in the crucible of the heart, forged in the heat of desire,
Burning with the warmth of a soul's deepest wish, yet cooling into the cold silence of unspoken thoughts.
Within these pages lies the essence of humanity.
Our loves that soar like birds on a wind too swift to capture,
Our losses that fall like ash from the heavens, settling into our bones,
Our endless yearning for meaning, for something more than this fleeting existence,

A longing that stretches beyond the stars, seeking connection in the dark.
Drink deeply, wanderer, and let the whispers guide you
through the fog of your own uncertainties,
For in the cauldron's depths, the soul's fire burns eternal,
Flickering through the veils of time, beckoning those brave enough to face its glow,
To look beyond the horizon, to follow the call of the unseen,
To hear, at last, the truth that lies hidden beneath the surface of the world.
So step forward, and let the cauldron's mysteries shape you,
For what lies within these pages is not just a collection of words,
But a journey, a revelation, a dance between the light and the dark,
A spell that will bind your spirit to the pulse of the universe itself.

1. WHEN WE EMBRACE

I don't know where or when we'll meet,
But I feel every part of me drawn to you.
In your thoughts, the shadows retreat,
As the light of love breaks through.
Love transcends both time and space,
For a hundred lifetimes, and a hundred more,
I've written this poem, a timeless trace,
So we can read it together once more.
I'm certain that somewhere, in some embrace,
Our souls will find a way to soar

2. BANISHING DARKNESS

In my darkest thoughts,
I'll no longer dwell.
For in the depths of my heart,
I hold the key to my well.
Chains of worry and shackles of pain,
In the prison of my mind,
I'll break free from the strain.
With courage and hope,
I rise from despair;
Darkness, be gone
You no longer share.
I reclaim my light,
No longer defined;
In the strength of my spirit,
I leave fear behind.

3. ETHICAL EFFECTS

Someday our shadows
Will catch up with us,
Swallowing sunlight,
Dispersing curses
Like deathly dew drops
On untouched roses.

4. UNLUCKY CURSE

The knife of betrayal Sharp and sleek.
Strikes in silence when the heart is weak.
Then the game of trust; The highest cost Is not what is gained
When it's me you've lost.
Cursed by luck Like depths unseen.
Where light can't reach, Where air grows lean.
In this spell I seek to brake
The suffocating holds of luckless lake.
Breathe again in freedom's air
In a life more just in fair.
Bad luck chains now decompose
In fortunes light, I now repose

5. SINISTER INVOCATION

From the vast universe,
to this space I'm in.
I beckon the forces,
let the good luck begin.
With every sunrise and each star's light fall I am favoured,
I am blessed, i receive the call.
Spirals of smoke, from incense so sweet.
Carry my wishes, make them complete.
For every obstacle a door shall appear, Guided by luck, my path becomes clear.
By day and by night, by dark and by light,
Fortune's embrace; holds me tight.
As I end this chant; with my heart so free,
So mote it be,
let it be, blessed be.

6. ASHES REBORN

They burned and
exhaled us to the shadows.
But from the ashes, we raise
thought they could, extinguish our flames.
But in their ignorance, They only fueled our eternal enrange.

7. IATRIC DWELL

From the universe's vast; infinite well, Draw the power where healing dwells.
Restore balance, inside and out, In health and wholeness, without a doubt.
With this spell, I call to mend,
To body and soul, let wellness extend.
In harmony with nature's embrace, Wrapped in healing, wrapped in grace.

8. WAKE YOU IN DREAM

As flame lights shadow,
And truth ends fear.
Open locked thoughts,
To my mind's willing ears.
May the smoke from this candle into Everywhere creep.
Bringing innermost voices, my mind in speech.

9. OUT OF VENOUS CLAWS

I release the ties, that once held tight.
Freeing myself from their venomous bite.
No longer will their negativity surround
As I cleanse my energy, firm and profound.
I am a fortress, strong and secure Shielded
from toxicity, light and pure. I draw boundaries, firm and clear.
Protecting my well-being
without fear.

10. SANGUINEM LUNA

Blood moon hign in the night sky,
Crimson glow of transformation night.
I release what no longer serves,
Embrace and change my soul preserves.
Old patterns and habits fade away,
In your power I find my sway.
Blood moon, guide me through; Transformation strong and true

11. COR GLACIEI

Ice and Frost take,
Cold tonight.
Freeze the night, Uphold the right.
May harm no pass, Nor malic stir.
Still the words with Winter's fur,
As the water turns to ice.
Halt the harm, Entrap the vice.

12. FLAMMAE KARMA

In the flames of "karma"

Were destinies ignite.

I call upon its power, It's formidable might. May the fires of retribution;

be fair and just burn away fast,

and turn them to dust.

For every action shall, equal just return.

In the fires of karma let this lesson burn.

13. MEUM EST

In the realm of the taken,
Where losses reside.
I cast the spell with, Power and pride,
To reclaim what's mine.
I invoke the spell, With it i trust.
I call upon forces, And let truth shine.
In the balance of justice, I take back what's mine.

14. UMBRA INFORTUNII

In the cold of the night,
where shadows dwell
I cast the spell to, brake and repel.
By the light of the stars, so distant and bright.
Dispel the shadow, bring forth the light.
With bad luck banished, My path is clear.
There lies a journey, Free from fear.

15. MID NIGHT WALK

Uncleed memories of Broken lights Knuckles sore with empty fights.
I blew a hole in the wall; To see if you were still On the other side.
But accidentally opened a portal
To the grave yard;
And the stench of rotting flesh
Filled my mind.

16. Incantatio Divitiarum

Golden streams, abundance flow,
Seeds of fortune, let them grow.
By the moon and sunlit gleam,
Manifest my prospering dream.
Coins of silver, gold, and green,
Fill my path, unseen, serene.
Open doors where riches lie,
With gratitude, my spirits fly

17. Incantatio Postscenium

Behind the curtain's heavy veil,
Where whispers dance, and stories sail,
A world unseen begins to hum,
The heart of theater beats its drum.
The walls hold secrets, old and new,
Dreams of triumph, moments few,
Echoes linger in shadowed halls,
Of laughter's rise and curtain calls.
Costumes shimmer in muted light,
Props await their turn to ignite,
Scripts, like spells, their magic weave,
Transforming minds that dare believe.
The cast, like alchemists, prepare,
To turn the ordinary into rare,
Breathing life into penned-down lore,
Opening unseen, enchanted doors.
Oh, back stage realm of raw emotion,
A sacred sea of boundless motion,
You hold the spell that makes us see,
The power of art, the joy to be

18. BINDING OF SOULS

By the fire's gentle glow,
And the rivers as they flow,
I call upon the forces near,
To draw you close, to bring you here.
With every breath, with every sigh,
Let our souls be bound, you and I.
Under moonlight's tender gaze,
We'll kindle love that never fades.
Through time and space, our hearts entwine,
Your spirit echoes deep in mine.
No harm, no chains, no shadows cast,
Just love, eternal, pure, and vast.
As stars align in heaven's embrace,
Bring us together, heart and face.
So mote it be, this love shall stay,
A bond unbroken, come what may.

19. Curse of Shadows

In the still of night, beneath the moon's pale gleam,
I weave a spell from the darkest dream.
Threads of wrath, with vengeance tied,
To strike my foe, where shadows abide.
By earth and fire, by water and air,
Let their spirit falter, their strength impair.
May their steps be heavy, their will undone,
As fate decrees, their time is run.
But heed this warning, the cost you bear,
For spells of malice tread despair.
Linger not long in hatred's art,
Lest it claim your soul, your very heart

20. Spell of Heartwarming

With gentle whispers, soft and true,
A warmth begins, it flows to you.
Through open hearts and hands that care,
Kindness lingers, fills the air.
By fire's glow and love's embrace,
Let joy alight on every face.
A healing spark, a tender art,
This spell ignites the human heart.

21. The Veil of Shadows

Under moonlight's cold embrace,
A shadow rises, leaving no trace.
From ashes dark, I weave my art,
Binding souls, tearing worlds apart.
Ten raven feathers, blood of night,
Bring forth the wraith from endless blight.
It whispers truths of darkened lore,
Secrets lost in ages' core.
With this chant, the veil shall part,
And shadows reign in every heart.

22. The Crimson Bloom

O rose of blood, in twilight bloom,
Unfold your petals, scent of doom.
From thorn to flesh, your venom spread,
A bond between the living and the dead.
With silver chalice, drink the wine,
Blended with poison, sharp and divine.
As veins turn black and vision fades,
New life springs where death invades.
A blooming curse, a deadly art,
To claim the soul, to steal the heart

23. The Call of the Abyss

Below the waves where light won't shine,
The abyss stirs, a force divine.
With whispered tones and ancient rune,
Awake the beast beneath the moon.
Salt and bone, the chant begins,
Binding flesh to oceans' sins.
A tidal surge, a siren's cry,
The waters rise, the heavens die.
O power deep, now hear my plea,
Unleash the storm; bring them to me

24. The Cursed Mirror

In glass so black, reflections fade,
A soul ensnared, a pact is made.
Speak thy name, and bind it tight,
To the endless void of endless night.
Silvered shards hold truths untold,
The mirror's grip is dark and cold.
Show the past, reveal the lies,
Let shadows bleed from staring eyes.
The price is steep, the toll is near,
A life for a glance, a soul for fear.

25. The Eternal Flame

By ember's glow and coal's embrace,
I summon fire from time and space.
A spark to burn, a blaze to grow,
Consume the earth, and lay it low.
By candle's wick and phoenix's tear,
This flame shall thrive and conquer fear.
No rain can quench, no wind can halt,
Its hunger burns without a fault.
O eternal fire, rise and see,
A world remade in ash for me

26. The Blackened Crown

Forge from iron, dipped in night,
A crown to hold infernal might.
With every thorn, a promise sworn,
To claim the skies and rise reborn.
By dragon's breath and devil's ire,
Fuel the forge with cursed fire.
Let kings and queens their thrones deny,
For this crown shall rule the sky.
Its wearer's fate is blood and flame,
A sovereign born of fear and shame on

27. The Harp of Sorrow

Strings of silver, cold as frost,
Play melodies of all I've lost.
A tune to bind, a hymn to rend,
The living's will to sorrow bend.
Each note a tear, each chord a cry,
To summon spirits where shadows lie.
A harp that calls the restless dead,
To haunt the living, to weave their dread.
Strike the chord, let the darkness sing,
A dirge of grief, a haunting sting

28. The Midnight Pact

Under stars in endless sprawl,
I make my plea, I give my call.
By serpent's fang and raven's wing,
I bind myself to the eternal king.
A circle drawn in dust and bone,
No spell undone, no curse unknown.
Let winds howl and thunder roar,
Seal this bond forevermore.
In midnight's grasp, I place my soul,
To gain the dark and pay the toll

29. The Blood Moon's Cry

When crimson moon lights up the sky,
The time has come for souls to die.
With dagger sharp and whispered vow,
Bring forth the beast; release it now.
From human shell to feral shape,
The curse shall bloom, there's no escape.
The forest stirs, the hunt begins,
A night of chaos, primal sins.
Under the blood moon, creatures rise,
The wild unleashed, the savage cries

30. The Frostbound Curse

O winter winds, so cruel and cold,
Turn flesh to ice, let frost take hold.
With snowflake sharp and frozen breath,
I conjure forth a living death.
A frozen world, a lifeless keep,
A kingdom locked in eternal sleep.
Ice for fire, chill for heat,
A curse unbroken, bitter, complete.
Let the frost consume and grow,
Until the earth is blank with snow.

31. The Pact

Under the moon, I etched his name,
A pact of fire, eternal flame.
Blood on stone, the circle drawn,
Life for power before the dawn.
His eyes of coal, his voice a knife,
"Give your soul; I'll grant you life."
Whispers weave through midnight air,
The devil's grin, a fatal snare.
In shadows deep, I made my vow,
Forever his, I'm burning now.

32. The Devil's Call

Ashes rise as candles burn,
A soul condemned shall not return.
Chant the verse, the ancient rhyme,
Open wide the gates of time.
"Lucifer, I summon thee,
Grant me power, set me free!"
But freedom's price is always steep,
A promise bound I cannot keep.
The devil laughs as darkness falls,
Forever cursed by his cruel calls.

33. A Devil's Trade

Blackened tome, forbidden spell,
The words unlock the gates of hell.
By the horns and serpent's breath,
I call the king who brings forth death!
The earth did quake, the air grew thin,
His claws reached out to draw me in.
"Riches, fame—what will it be?"
I spoke my wish, "Eternity."
A crooked smile, his trade was done,
My soul consumed before the sun.

34. Infernal Bond

Through smoke and flame, I carved a sigil,
A mark to bind the devil's vigil.
With sulfur's scent and iron blade,
The crimson deal was swiftly made.
"Bring me strength, my darkest lord,
Break the chains, unleash the horde!"
But power's cost, I soon would learn,
A devil's gift is no one's to spurn.
Bound in chains of burning pain,
I walk his path, a life profane.

35. The Devil's Game

Beneath the stars, a deck was dealt,
His eyes like fire, his power felt.
Cards of fate, each choice a sin,
The devil smiled, "Shall we begin?"
I gambled time, I gambled soul,
I sought the prize, a heart made whole.
But every card, a darker play,
The devil's hand would win the day.
Now in his grasp, I'm forced to stay,
A pawn within his endless sway.

36. Hellbound Rhyme

In cursed rhyme, his name I spoke,
And with that word, the air grew choked.
A blazing form, both cruel and tall,
His laugh resounded through the hall.
"Why summon me, you foolish child?
Do you not fear the fire wild?"
"I seek revenge," I boldly said,
"Make my enemies wish they were dead."
He laughed again, my soul he claimed,
Now bound to him, my life defamed.

37. Shadow's Whisper

Under the oak, I dug the grave,
To call the one who does not save.
A vial of blood, a strand of hair,
I whispered his name into the air.
The ground did quake, the roots did writhe,
The devil rose with claws and scythe.
"Your wish is mine, but know the price,
A soul once pure, now turned to ice."
His whispers haunt me every night,
A deal with him brings endless fright.

38. The Devil's Mirror

A mirror framed in cursed gold,
Reflected secrets never told.
I lit the flame, I spoke the spell,
And conjured forth the king of hell.
"Reveal the truths, the paths I seek,
Grant me strength to harm the weak!"
But in that glass, his face appeared,
With every word, my fate was seared.
Now trapped within the mirror's gleam,
Forever lost in a devil's dream.

39. Serpent's Song

Through forest dark, to chapel old,
I sang the hymn of spirits cold.
"Lucifer, O prince of night,
Grant me vengeance, grant me might!"
The serpent came, its tongue a flame,
It whispered soft and called my name.
"What you wish, I shall provide,
But tread with care, your soul's my bride."
Its song now echoes in my veins,
A devil's curse, eternal chains.

40. Candlelight Curse

Nine black candles, burning bright,
A spell to call infernal might.
"By the horns and cloven feet,
I summon thee to make me complete!"
The devil came, his grin obscene,
A shadowed lord, both fierce and lean.
"Speak your wish; the price is steep,"
I spoke, "To dream while others sleep."
Now haunted dreams are all I find,
A devil's curse binds soul and mind

41. Shadow's Call

Beneath the moon's dim, silver light,
Summon shadows from the night.
Speak their names, the whispers grow,
Binding darkness to your soul.
Light a flame and snuff it out,
Fill the air with fear and doubt.
The world will shake, the stars will weep,
As darkness rises from the deep.
Beware the cost, the soul's frail tether,
For shadows stay with you forever

42. Fire's Hunger

Chant to flames that ever burn,
Ask their favor, ask in turn.
Cast a spark into the air,
Let it catch, and let it flare.
Speak of vengeance, speak of pain,
The fire will consume your chain.
Once unleashed, it will not rest,
Until it scorches all the west.
Fire hungers, fire feeds,
On mortal greed and wicked deeds.

43. Blood's Binding

Draw a circle, painted red,
With lifeblood from the vein you've bled.
Speak the name of what you seek,
Its shadow stirs, its presence leaks.
Give an oath, your soul in trade,
The pact is sealed, the deal is made.
But blood remembers, blood collects,
Every sin it resurrects.
What you gain is what you lose,
A devil's price you cannot refuse

44. Storm's Wrath

Call the thunder, call the rain,
Let your voice evoke their bane.
Strike the ground and raise the sky,
Let the tempest amplify.
Speak the winds, demand their rage,
Unleash them from their timeless cage.
But storms are wild, storms betray,
What they grant, they take away.
So wield their power, but beware,
The storm leaves none of its victims spared.

45. Mirror's Curse

Gaze into the glassy sheen,
Find the devil, sharp and keen.
Speak to it, your darker twin,
Let it guide the curse within.
Twist the image, twist the light,
To steal another's will or sight.
But mirrors show the truth concealed,
What's done to others is revealed.
For every curse, a cost is weighed,
And mirrored sins are never stayed.

46. Time's Undoing

Turn the clock, let time rewind,
To steal the moments left behind.
Speak the spell to halt the flow,
Or speed it up for what you know.
But time is jealous, time is sly,
What you alter, it will defy.
Twisting threads, it weaves anew,
A fate more twisted comes to you.
For every second that you gain,
A devil waits to stake its claim.

47. Night's Whisper

Speak the words the night conceals,
Let it grant the truths it steals.
Ask the stars to light your path,
Though their wisdom stirs their wrath.
The whispers come, soft and sweet,
With secrets stolen, incomplete.
But nights are long, and truths are dire,
They burn the soul like starlit fire.
Once you hear, you can't un-know,
The devil's whisper leaves its woe

48. Stone's Command

Touch the earth and call its might,
Raise the mountains, crush the fight.
Speak to stone, its heart will yield,
Turn it into blade and shield.
But earth is stubborn, earth is slow,
Its weight a burden you will know.
Once it moves, it cannot stop,
It claims the weak, it claims the top.
The devil waits in rock and clay,
To take your life another day.

49. Soul's Reflection

Look within and chant the phrase,
Find the devil in the maze.
Speak your wish and hold its hand,
Let it guide you through the land.
But what it shows is not your fate,
It tricks the mind, deceives the gate.
Your soul it twists, your will it breaks,
With every choice the demon takes.
To seek yourself, you must beware,
The devil's touch is always there.

50. Whispers of the Mausoleum

Beneath the moon's pale, lifeless gaze,
Stone angels weep in hollow haze.
The crypt breathes cold, its shadows creep,
A sepulcher where secrets sleep.
Faint whispers echo through the air,
Lost voices chant a ghostly prayer.
Vines strangle headstones in their clutch,
Time's cruel hand leaves all in rust.
Night's shroud descends, the past awakes,
A fleeting chill, the silence breaks.
Here death is not a quiet end—
It lingers, haunting, as a friend.

51. The Portrait's Curse

Her eyes, a depthless, glassy stare,
Locked forever in her painter's care.
The brush had bound her soul to frame,
A beauty caught in art's cruel game.
At dusk, she stirs, her whispers call,
Her voice a dirge through empty halls.
She weeps for love and blood she lacks,
A phantom bound, she can't turn back.
Her shadow dances on the floor,
While footsteps echo evermore.
In the canvas, life and death entwine—
A timeless curse, a vengeful shrine.

52. The Bleeding Rose

In the garden of the dead, it grows,
A crimson bloom, the bleeding rose.
Its petals drip with tears of red,
Each drop a life the thorn has fed.
Under a sky so bleak and grey,
The rose devours the light of day.
Its fragrance lures both man and beast,
A poison sweet, a deadly feast.
Yet once you pluck it from the vine,
Your soul becomes the rose's shrine.
Beware the bloom that haunts the glen,
Its beauty damns both gods and men.

53. The Clock Strikes None

In the tower where the gears unwind,
A clock ticks on, but time's confined.
Its face is cracked, its hands are still,
Yet whispers flow, a ghostly chill.
Each chime recalls a shadowed past,
A moment lost, yet cursed to last.
The keeper, pale, with hollowed eyes,
Winds the clock with endless sighs.
The hours pass but never fade,
For time itself this curse betrayed.
An endless loop, a timeless pain,
Bound to the tower's dark domain

54. The Candle's Lament

A single flame in endless night,
Its flicker casts a ghostly light.
It weeps with wax, a silent cry,
A fleeting life doomed to die.
Each shadow birthed upon the wall,
Carries whispers of the fall.
The candle knows it cannot last,
Yet clings to hope, though time moves fast.
A glimmer bright in cold decay,
Its embers fade, the dark will stay.
For light must die where shadows loom,
And leave the world to endless gloom.

55. The Chapel of Ash

Beneath the spire of broken dreams,
The chapel stands in moonlit beams.
Its pews are blackened, carved with pain,
Its altar stained by sorrow's rain.
The air is thick with prayers unspoken,
Faith long lost, its chains now broken.
No choir sings, no candles burn,
Only shadows in silence turn.
Yet spirits linger, kneel, and mourn,
For something sacred, long forlorn.
In ash and ruin, hope resides,
A fragile light where darkness hides.

56. The Raven Queen

Upon her throne of shattered stone,
The Raven Queen rules all alone.
Her crown is forged of night's despair,
Her gown is stitched from shadows' glare.
Her voice commands the winds to weep,
Her gaze pulls stars from heavens deep.
A thousand souls her courtly feast,
Bound to her will, they serve the beast.
She whispers truths none dare to hear,
Each word a blade that cuts with fear.
Beware her wings, her endless flight,
She is the empress of the night

57. The Gravekeeper's Vigil

He walks among the silent dead,
His lantern glow a ghostly red.
Each grave he tends with solemn care,
A guardian of despair.
His shadow stretches long and thin,
A specter born of guilt within.
By day, he fades, a mortal guise,
By night, the truth in darkness lies.
For he is neither flesh nor bone,
A keeper bound to worlds unknown.
Forever trapped to serve and mourn,
A soul lost in the twilight born.

58. The Ghost in the Mirror

A visage stares, but not my own,
Eyes like stars, yet cold as stone.
Her hand reaches from silver's sheen,
A haunting beauty, cruel and keen.
Each glance reveals a fleeting tear,
A life unlived, consumed by fear.
She whispers truths that twist the mind,
A pact of blood, a fate unkind.
Her touch is ice, her breath a storm,
Her love a curse, her kiss transforms.
Beware the mirror's darkened pane,
It holds your soul in shadow's chain.

59. The Organ's Dirge

The organ sighs in haunting tone,
A melody of grief unknown.
Its pipes breathe dust, its keys are worn,
A requiem for hearts forlorn.
Each note resounds through empty aisles,
A symphony of sorrowed trials.
Its player sits, a phantom gray,
Lost in music night and day.
No mortal hears the dirge's cry,
Yet spirits gather, drawn nearby.
For in its chords, the dead arise,
To dance beneath the moonlit skies.

60. The Devil's Whisper

In shadows deep where darkness falls,
The devil whispers through the walls.
With hollow eyes and twisted grin,
He beckons souls, to sink in sin.
A clawed hand reaches, cold as stone,
Luring the lost to realms unknown.
In whispered lies, his voice does weave,
And souls succumb, in him they believe.
The moon hangs low, its light does die,
As hellish flames kiss the night sky.
Beware the devil, his kiss is sweet,
But his embrace is death's deceit.

61. Crimson Eyes

The devil's eyes, a burning red,
Where countless souls have long since fled.
He watches, waiting, cold and still,
To break the will and twist the will.
His wings of ash and iron claws,
Bring doom with every darkened pause.
Upon the earth, he walks in gloom,
Turning hope to certain doom.
His laughter rings in the wind's chill air,
The devil's grip is everywhere.
In every shadow, he shall find,
The deepest fear that haunts the mind.

62. The Devil's Dance

In the moon's pale, twisted light,
The devil waltzes through the night.
With fiery steps on cursed ground,
He spins and dances, no sound.
His footfalls echo in the dark,
A twisted, evil, chilling spark.
He calls to those who lose their way,
To join his dance and never stray.
Beneath his feet, the earth shall break,
For in his step, the heavens quake.
In endless twirls and ghastly trance,
The devil leads the cursed dance.

63. Satan's Crown

Upon his head, a crown of flame,
The devil calls, and none can tame.
A kingdom built on pain and fear,
Where tortured screams are all you hear.
His throne is made of ash and stone,
A seat of torment, made his own.
His heart is black, his soul a void,
Where endless cries are all destroyed.
He rules in shadows, far away,
Where hope and light have gone astray.
The devil's reign will never cease,
For he shall rule with no release.

64. In the Devil's Grasp

A whispered promise in the night,
The devil calls with burning light.
His hands are cold, yet pull you near,
Into a world of endless fear.
His breath is poison, sharp as steel,
A grip so tight, you cannot heal.
His laughter rings through every bone,
The devil claims you as his own.
No prayers, no tears, no mortal plea,
Can set your spirit ever free.
The devil smiles and pulls you down,
To wear eternity's dark crown.

65. The Infernal Pact

A bargain struck in deepest night,
The devil offers you his might.
A golden promise, dark and sweet,
For souls to sacrifice and greet.
A soul for power, wealth, and fame,
In his foul name, you'll play the game.
Yet in his eyes, a fire burns,
As you begin to feel the churn.
For every wish, a cost is paid,
As every deal in shadows laid.
In the devil's grasp, you'll never flee,
For in the dark, you cease to be.

66. The Devil's Garden

In the devil's garden, flowers grow,
With petals black and hearts aglow.
The scent of death fills every breeze,
A deadly calm upon the trees.
His creatures crawl, with eyes of flame,
Whispering softly, calling your name.
The grass is cold, the skies are torn,
A garden where the dead are born.
Yet still you wander, lost in trance,
Caught in the devil's cursed dance.
In the garden, there's no escape,
For here, your soul he'll soon reshape.

67. Beneath the Devil's Wing

Beneath the devil's twisted wing,
The world shall weep and angels sing.
A tear of blood, a cry of pain,
Where innocence is born of bane.
He walks in silence, steps of dread,
His heart beats not, his soul is dead.
Yet still he hunts, with cunning grin,
To feast upon the souls of sin.
A lord of lies, a king of wrath,
He guides you down the cursed path.
Beneath his wing, no light shall gleam,
Only shadows that haunt your dream.

68. The Devil's Throne

Upon a throne of ash and flame,
The devil sits, a lord of shame.
His crown is made of souls he's claimed,
A throne, where no one's safe or named.
His eyes are endless, dark as night,
He watches with infernal might.
The earth trembles beneath his gaze,
As darkness spreads in endless haze.
He speaks no word, yet all must hear,
His whispers fed on endless fear.
In his kingdom, hope is torn,
For the devil reigns, and souls are worn.

69. In the Devil's Eyes

Within the devil's eyes you'll see,
A world of pain and misery.
A place where angels fear to tread,
Where joy is lost, and hope is dead.
His gaze, a poison to the mind,
A fire that burns, but leaves behind.
He seeks no love, he feels no grief,
Only hunger, and endless thief.
In his eyes, you'll see your end,
A soul to break, a will to bend.
For in the devil's stare you'll find,
The depths of hell within your mind.

70. The Lady of the Veil

She stands beneath the weeping tree,
A veil of shadows hides her eyes.
The moonlight glimmers cold and free,
A mystery beneath the skies.
Her whispers call through endless night,
A chill that makes the heart take flight.
Her breath is heavy, her smile pale,
A haunting ghost, a wind-blown wail.
She walks among the graveyard stones,
Her footsteps echo with old moans.
The night embraces her like a shroud,
The Lady whispers, soft and loud.

71. The Widow's Grief

Beneath the crypt, she mourns alone,
A widow dressed in black and bone.
Her tears like pearls, they stain her face,
She weeps for love she can't replace.
The crows above in silence stand,
While death holds her with cold, dead hand.
Her heart is hollow, dark and deep,
A memory she cannot keep.
In silence, she lays down her plea,
For him to rise and set her free.
But in the grave, her love remains,
A widow's sorrow, endless chains

72. The Ghost in the Mirror

She stands behind the glass so still,
Her face a pale and hollow chill.
Her eyes, like voids, reflect no light,
A specter trapped in endless night.
Her lips, they form a soundless plea,
A soul confined, forever free.
She reaches out but cannot touch,
A reflection that hurts too much.
Her shadow, lost in time's cruel maze,
Her spirit bound in mirrored gaze.
The glass may break, but she will stay,
The ghost within, forever gray.

73. The Witch's Song

A melody hums in the midnight air,
A woman's voice beyond compare.
Her lips, like petals, soft and sweet,
Enchant the night with rhythmic beat.
Her words, they twist with ancient power,
A spell to call the witching hour.
Her eyes, like fire, burn with glee,
And all who hear are doomed to see.
She dances in the storm's embrace,
Her magic, dark, her skin a trace.
The moonlight flickers, shadows crawl,
Her voice, a curse, to end it all.

74. The Lost Maiden

In the forest, a maiden weeps,
Her heart, like a secret, buried deep.
The trees, they whisper tales of woe,
Of love she lost so long ago.
Her hair is dark, her skin so pale,
Her sorrow woven into her veil.
She wanders through the endless night,
Her eyes reflecting no daylight.
The wind may call, but she won't hear,
For silence is her deepest fear.
A maiden lost to time and tears,
Her soul trapped here for endless years.

75. The Queen of Shadows

Her crown is made of twisted night,
A queen who reigns in dim moonlight.
Her gaze is cold, her smile a lie,
A monarch beneath a weeping sky.
Her robes are woven with despair,
A shroud of darkness in the air.
She rules with hands so pale, so cold,
A heart that's lost, a soul so old.
The realm she walks is full of gloom,
A shadowed kingdom, endless tomb.
Her throne is built from broken dreams,
A queen of night, where nothing gleams

76. The Pale Maiden

A pale maiden walks through the mist,
Her lips, a crimson kiss dismissed.
Her feet, they leave no mark or trace,
As if the earth won't dare to chase.
Her hair, like silver, winds and sways,
She walks through endless nights and days.
Her eyes are lost in a distant land,
Her heart is bound by death's cold hand.
She seeks the light but finds no grace,
Her shadow is her only face.
A pale maiden, with time so cruel,
Her beauty lost, her spirit a fool

77. The Veiled Sorceress

Beneath the veil, her eyes do burn,
A thousand secrets twist and turn.
Her hands are pale, but full of might,
A sorceress in the dead of night.
She calls to shadows, whispers low,
Her power, like the river's flow.
Her lips, they speak the words of doom,
That fill the air with endless gloom.
Her magic flows like blood, so black,
A curse that never turns back.
The veil she wears, a binding spell,
A sorceress, born to quell.

78. The Dark Siren

Upon the rocks, she sings so sweet,
A siren with no voice to greet.
Her song, it beckons sailors near,
To pull them into death's cold sphere.
Her eyes, like oceans, dark and deep,
She holds them close, they never sleep.
Her hair, like waves, it crashes high,
A storm beneath the moonlit sky.
Her touch is cold, her heart is ice,
She lures them in with deadly vice.
The waves embrace her with a cry,
A siren's song, a sailor's die.

79. The Doll's Curse

She sits in silence, stiff and still,
A doll with glassy eyes to fill.
Her porcelain skin, so smooth and fair,
But there's a darkness in the air.
Her lips don't move, her heart is stone,
A curse that makes her feel alone.
Her hands are frozen in a pose,
Her life a prison none will know.
She dreams of freedom, of the sun,
But knows her fate cannot be undone.
A doll she seems, but cursed to last,
A soul that's trapped in shadows' grasp.

80. The Bloodstained Night

The moon hung high, a pale, cruel gaze,
As shadows danced in endless haze.
A dagger gleamed with wicked grace,
As I struck down in cold embrace.
The crimson spilled, a river deep,
Into the earth, where secrets sleep.
A whispered curse upon the air,
A soul departed, unaware.
I walk the night with bloodied hands,
A murderer of darkened lands.
The killing, though, a tale untold,
Will echo in the winds so cold.

81. The Silent Requiem

In silence, death, a final breath,
A kiss of cold, a dance with death.
The whispered plea, the soul that cried,
But in my heart, no tears reside.
A blade, so sharp, so pure, so bright,
Takes life away and ends the night.
A whisper in the winds does fade,
The soul condemned, the price is paid.
The echoes of the fall remain,
A haunting, never-ending stain.
In shadows deep, I stand alone,
The blood of innocence my throne

82. The Crimson Vow

By candlelight, a promise made,
To see the final breath decayed.
In whispers soft, a fate is sealed,
A life to take, a wound to heal.
A heart once pure, now stained with sin,
The darkness waits to pull within.
The dagger sings its lullaby,
As innocence begins to die.
A vow to end what once was kind,
The crimson stain that fills my mind.
The world shall mourn, but I shall smile,
For death, to me, is but a trial

83. The Hollow Cry

A scream, a plea, a soul betrayed,
In shadows deep, the price is paid.
A hand that strikes, a heart that falls,
The silence echoes through the halls.
A soul departed, never more,
Its body slumped on cold, dark floor.
The hollow cry, it haunts my mind,
As guilt and madness intertwine.
Each step I take, each breath I steal,
I wonder if this pain is real.
For every life that I have claimed,
A thousand more will bear my name.

84. The Final Dance

A waltz, so slow, beneath the moon,
A deadly tune, a haunting rune.
The blade, so sharp, it sings its song,
As death and life together belong.
A whisper soft, a touch so cold,
A kiss of death that takes its hold.
The body falls, its breath is gone,
A soul now lost, a life withdrawn.
In shadows deep, I dance with death,
Each step a snuffing out of breath.
For in this waltz, I am the king,
And death, my crown, forever rings.

85. The Mourning Bell

The bell tolls loud, a bitter sound,
As death descends without a bound.
A life erased, a soul erased,
A victim left, forever chased.
A cold embrace, a final sigh,
Beneath the moonless, sable sky.
The shadows stretch, the blade does gleam,
As nightmares dance, and hope does scream.
I walk the path of blood and bone,
The killing done, the debt is known.
But when the bell begins to toll,
It calls for me, to take its toll.

86. The Darkened Throne

A shadowed king, with hands of night,
His heart as cold as endless fright.
He takes the lives, he takes the souls,
For in his court, there are no roles.
The bloodstained floor, the crimson wall,
Each life he claims, another falls.
A whisper soft, a fatal plea,
But none can flee his dark decree.
Upon his throne, he rests alone,
For he has made the world his own.
The killing, though, is just the start;
A kingdom ruled by broken hearts.

87. The Widow's Lament

A life, a love, so dearly lost,
A soul now bound by death's cruel cost.
I take the knife, I take the aim,
For in this world, I'll find my claim.
The blood, it stains my hands so red,
The man I killed, now cold and dead.
Yet in my heart, no joy resides,
Only a sorrow that never hides.
The widow's lament, it fills the air,
For death has shown no mercy, fair.
But in the night, the killing's sweet,
As fate and I in shadows meet.

88. The Dark Harvest

The harvest comes, the reaper's call,
As death descends upon us all.
With sickle sharp and eyes of dread,
I reap the souls, I leave them dead.
The earth shall drink the blood it craves,
As I walk through a thousand graves.
No prayer, no plea, no final word,
For death will not be long deterred.
The harvest dark, the crops of doom,
Shall flower in the world's own tomb.
For every life I take, I sow,
A garden where the dark winds blow.

89. Death's Embrace

The final breath, so soft, so sweet,
A death so quiet, none shall greet.
A hand that falls, a heart that stills,
As life is lost to death's dark wills.
The body slumps, the soul takes flight,
Into the endless, endless night.
But I remain, a killer bold,
A heart that's dark, a soul so cold.
The last breath gone, the darkness grows,
But in my mind, the killing flows.
For death is not an end, but start,
A curse upon my wicked heart.

90. The Last Breath

Call the reaper, call the blade,
To bring the end for which you prayed.
Speak the words, a solemn plea,
To summon death from shadowed sea.
But death is fickle, death is sly,
It questions who and wonders why.
For every soul it takes away,
Another price you'll have to pay.
So tread with care, and weigh your fears,
The devil dances where death appears.

Author's Note

WHISPERS OF THE CAULDRON is a journey into the depths of the mystical, where shadows and light dance in an eternal waltz. As a writer, I have always been fascinated by the stories and secrets that lie beyond the surface of our everyday lives. This collection is a reflection of those whispered tales, drawn from folklore, myth, and the untold wonders of the human spirit.

Each poem in this book emerges from the cauldron of imagination, where the raw, often chaotic elements of emotion, wisdom, and history swirl together. The cauldron represents not only a place of transformation but also a symbol of the unknown, where truths are forged in fire, and magic is born.

Through these verses, I invite you to explore realms where the boundaries of time and space are blurred. The characters and creatures that inhabit these poems are not bound by the rules of reality, but instead are shaped by the universal forces of nature and spirit. They whisper ancient knowledge and speak truths that have been lost to time, yet are eternally relevant.

This book is my way of sharing a piece of my heart and mind with you. It is an offering to those who seek the unspoken, the unseen, and the mysterious. May you find, in these whispers, a connection to something larger than yourself—something that stirs the soul and beckons you to listen more closely to the world around you.

Thank you for stepping into this world with me, and for allowing the whispers to find their way into your heart.

With gratitude and wonder,

[S MAYUR]

pseudonym [KC]

www.ingramcontent.com/pod-product-compliance
Lightning Source LLC
La Vergne TN
LVHW091028150826
845672LV00006BA/1732

* 9 7 9 8 8 9 6 3 2 5 1 0 9 *